Bond

UP TO *SPEED*
English
Tests and Papers

9–10 years

Sarah Lindsay

Nelson Thornes

Published in 2013 by:
Nelson Thornes Ltd
Delta Place
27 Bath Road
CHELTENHAM
GL53 7TH
United Kingdom

13 14 15 16 17 / 10 9 8 7 6 5 4 3 2 1

A catalogue record for this book is available from the British Library

ISBN 978 1 4085 1886 1

Page make-up by OKS Prepress, India

Printed in China by 1010 Printing International Ltd

Acknowledgements

The author and the publisher would like to thank the following for
permission to reproduce material:

P12 'The Flea and the Sheep' by Leonardo da Vinci taken from *Fables
of Leonardo da Vinci* translated by Bruno Nardini. Published by
HarperCollins; p32 'Best Friends' by Bernard Young © Bernard Young.
Reproduced with the kind permission of the author; p44 'The Hook'
by Michael Rosen from *Scary Stories for 10 year olds* chosen by Helen
Paiba, published by Walker Books. Reproduced with the permission of
United Agents.

Every effort has been made to trace the copyright holders but if any have
been inadvertently overlooked the publisher will be pleased to make the
necessary arrangements at the first opportunity.

Introduction

The Bond *Up to Speed* series is a new addition to the Bond range of assessment papers, the number one series for the 11+, selective exams and general practice. Bond *Up to Speed* is carefully designed to support above and beyond the level provided in the regular Bond assessment range.

How does this book work?

The book contains two distinct sets of papers, along with full answers and a Progress Chart:

- Focus tests, accompanied by advice and directions, are focused on particular (and age-appropriate) English question types encountered in the 11+ and other exams. The questions are deliberately set at a less challenging level than the standard *Assessment Papers*. Each Focus test is designed to help a child 'catch' their level in a particular question type, and then gently raise it through the course of the test and the subsequent mixed papers.

- Mixed papers are longer tests containing a full range of English question types. These are designed to provide rigorous practice with less challenging questions, perhaps against the clock, in order to help children acquire and develop the necessary skills and techniques for 11+ success.

Full answers are provided for both types of test in the middle of the book.

How much time should the tests take?

The tests are for practice and to reinforce learning, and you may wish to test exam techniques and working to a set time limit. Using the Mixed papers, we would recommend that your child spends 50 minutes answering the 75 questions in each paper, plus 5 minutes for reading the comprehension extract.

You can reduce the suggested time by 5 minutes to practise working at speed.

Using the Progress Chart

The Progress Chart can be used to track Focus test and Mixed paper results over time to monitor how well your child is doing and identify any repeated problems in tackling the different question types.

Write each of these words correctly.

Look carefully at each word. Which sound in the word could be made with a different letter or letters?

1 sekond — *Second*

2 tuff — *tough*

3 mouthfull — *Mouthful*

4 jiraffe — *Giraffe*

5 sandel — *Sandal*

6 patturn — *pattern*

6

Change these words into their **singular** form.

7 cows — *cow*

8 churches — *Church*

9 boxes — *box*

10 horses — *horse*

11 bushes — *Bush*

12 bikes — *Bike*

Watch out! You don't always just need to remove the s.

6

Add the **prefix** *un* or *dis* to each of these words.

A prefix is added to the beginning of a word to change its meaning.

13 *Dis* honest

14 *Dis* believe

15 *Un* aware

16 *Dis* continue

17 *Un* important

18 *Un* well

6

4

Circle the words that have a soft g.

19–24   goat   magic   giant   giggle

        storage   imagine   jogger   grease

        plug   plunge   gravel   strange   **6**

Complete the word sums.

25   child + hood   = *Childhood*

26   home + less   = *Homeless*

27   entertain + ment = *Entertainment*

28   expense + ive   = *Exponseive*

29   forgive + able   = *Forgiveable*

30   lonely + ness   = *Lonelyness*   **6**

Rewrite these sentences changing them from **plural** to **singular**.

> When you have changed the nouns to their singular form, reread the sentence to check that it still all makes sense.

1 Jess loved reading the books on her shelf.

   Jess loved reading books from her shelf.

2 The windows needed painting before it rained.

   ~~It was~~

3 The tennis courts were in use.

4 The cats played with the escaped mice.

5 The dogs were barking at the postman.

6 The sheep called to their lambs.

6

Add the missing commas to these sentences.

> You put commas between items in a list.

7–8 The sandwich had ham cheese pickle and tomato in it.

9–10 I must remember to take my green towel swimming costume clear goggles and hairbrush tonight.

11–12 Jacob loves to play football swim run races and sleep!

6

Rewrite these sentences adding the missing capital letters.

> You need capital letters for proper nouns as well as at the beginning of sentences.

13 we are going to swansea on tuesday.

14 have you read *the secret garden*?

_____

15 look, i think we are flying over mount everest.

_____

16 miss morris wants to see freya and harry before they go home.

_____

17 shall we go to london to see the musical *billy elliot*?

_____

18 kyle's birthday is in march, one month before mine.

_____ (6)

Underline the main **clause** in each of these sentences.

> *A clause is a section of a sentence including a verb.*

19 The rain poured in through the open window on to the chair.

20 Tuhil forgot to write down his homework so he got into trouble.

21 The washing machine broke down, which upset my mum.

22 The dog was exhausted after his walk and slept for hours.

23 Aimee loved going to the cricket club and then walking home with her friends afterwards.

24 Simon painted the windows very carefully so paint wouldn't go on the glass. (6)

Add the missing punctuation at the end of each sentence.

25 When does this film finish_____

26 This is a great book_____

27 Can we go and watch the air show_____

28 Stop, don't move_____

29 Fantastic news_____

30 I wish my dad could see me run_____ (6)

> These sentences have full stops, question marks and exclamation marks missing.

Focus test 3 Grammar 1

Copy the **proper nouns**, adding the missing capital letters.

Proper nouns are names of people, places, days of the week and so on.

1–6
kite	princess caroline	egypt	feather
mr golding	cavern	bread	january
machine	tooting street	notebook	tuesday

_____   _____   _____

_____   _____   _____

6

Underline the **verb** in each of these sentences.

7   The bike skidded to a halt.

8   The blood drips from my nose.

9   I check information on the internet.

10   I lost my pencil case yesterday.

11   Tory cooks a cake every weekend.

12   The trees blew in the wind.

A verb is a doing or being word.

6

In each gap, add a **connective**.

A connective connects two sentences or clauses.

13   We must hurry _____ we will miss the bus.

14   I've packed my cheese sandwich _____ I mustn't forget a drink.

15   I suggest that you read this book _____ I know you would love it.

16   We are going to Portugal this summer _____ it should be warmer than here!

17   I ran too fast in the race _____ now my legs are really hurting!

18   My dog loves me _____ someone else offers him a bone.

6

Complete the table below.

Comparative adjectives compare two nouns. Superlative adjectives compare more than two nouns. Watch out for spelling changes.

19–24

	Comparative adjectives	Superlative adjectives
big		biggest
small		
happy	happier	
sad		

6

Circle the **preposition** in each of these sentences.

A preposition can give the position of something in relation to something else.

25 The dog was locked inside the kitchen.

26 The pony jumped over the hedge gracefully.

27 Dan put the remote on the television.

28 Oscar hid under his bed.

29 The car drove into the garage.

30 The diver swam below the coral reef.

6

Focus test 4   Vocabulary 1

Write an **antonym** for each of these words.

> An antonym is a word that has the opposite meaning to another word.

1 unkind   _____

2 correct   _____

3 thick   _____

4 strong   _____

5 full   _____

6 freeze   _____

○ 6

Write two **onomatopoeic** words that are associated with each of these things.

> An onomatopoeic word echoes a sound associated with its meaning.

7–8   fireworks   _____   _____

9–10   water   _____   _____

11–12 a dog   _____   _____

○ 6

Mix and match these words to make six **compound words**.

> A compound word is a word made up of two other words, for example toothbrush.

back   mark   hand   book   ground   shake   made

13–18 _____   _____   _____

       _____   _____   _____

○ 6

Write one word for each of these **definitions**. Each word begins with the letter k.

> A definition is the meaning of a word.

19 A room where food is prepared and dishes are washed. k_____

20 A unit of distance, 1000 metres. k_____

21 The hard joints where your fingers meet your hand. k_____

22 A large Australian animal. k_____

23 A type of skirt traditionally worn by Scotsmen. k_____

24 An organ in your body that produces urine. k_____ 6

With a line, match the word to the country from where you think it is borrowed.

> Some words we use are borrowed from other countries.

25 café

26 pizza   Italy

27 volcano   USA

28 boutique   France

29 moose

30 cheeseburger   6

The Flea and the Sheep – a fable

A flea, who lived in the smooth hair of a dog, one day noticed the pleasant smell of wool.

"What is going on?"

He gave a little jump and saw that his dog had gone to sleep leaning against the fleece of a sheep. 5

"That fleece is exactly what I need," said the flea. "It is thicker and softer, and above all safer. There is no risk of meeting dog's claws and teeth which go in search of me every now and then. And the sheep's wool will certainly feel more pleasant."

So without thinking too much about it, the flea moved house, leaping 10 from the dog's coat to the sheep's fleece. But the wool was thick, so thick and dense that it was not easy to penetrate the skin.

He tried and tried, patiently separating one strand from another, and laboriously making a way through. At last he reached the roots of the hair. But they were so close together they practically touched. The flea had not 15 even a tiny hole through which to attack the skin.

Tired, bathed in sweat and bitterly disappointed, the flea resigned himself to going back to the dog. But the dog had gone away.

Poor flea! He wept for days and days with regret for his mistake.

Leonardo da Vinci

Answer these questions.

1 Who is the main character in this story?

_____

_____

2–3 Why did the flea consider moving from the dog to the sheep? Give four reasons.

_____

4 By moving to the sheep's wool, what was the flea hoping to avoid?

_____

5–6 Write two problems the flea discovered about the sheep's wool.

_____

_____

7 Why was the flea trying to get to the sheep's skin?

_____

8–9 How do you think the flea felt when he discovered that the dog had moved away from the sheep? Use evidence from the passage to support your answer.

_____

_____

10–11 What, in the context of the passage, do the following words mean?

'dense' (line 12) _____

'laboriously' (line 14) _____

12–13 A fable has an underlying message in its story. What do you think the message of 'The Flea and the Sheep' is?

_____

_____

_____

14–15 Make up a modern-day situation where a similar message to the one found in the story of the flea and the sheep could apply.

_____

_____

_____

_____

Focus test 6   Spelling 2

Rewrite these words, adding the **suffix** *ing* to each one.

> **Watch out! Sometimes a change in the word is needed before adding the suffix.**

1 knock   _____

2 drag   _____

3 amuse   _____

4 trick   _____

5 circle   _____

6 whisper   _____

6

Match each of these words to a word with the same letter string but a different pronunciation.

> **The letter string will include a vowel.**

moustache   cough   tongue

weight   bruise   dove

7   height   _____

8   rough   _____

9   move   _____

10 catalogue   _____

11 backache   _____

12 guide   _____

6

Circle the silent letter in each of these words.

13 s c i e n c e   14 g n o m e

15 s i g n   16 t h u m b

17 s c e n e   18 c l i m b e r   **6**

Write the **plural** form of each of these **nouns**.

19 lunch   _____

20 dish   _____

21 office   _____

22 baby   _____

23 marble   _____

24 daisy   _____   **6**

Add the **prefix** *auto* or *bi* to each of these words.

25 _____graph

26 _____plane

27 _____cycle

28 _____cue

29 _____pilot

30 _____annual   **6**

Rewrite each sentence as if you were writing about yourself.

> **Both the pronoun and verb might need changing.**

1 She enjoys reading. _____

2 He walks to school. _____

3 They eat tea at 6pm. _____

4 He woke up late. _____

5 She runs fast. _____

6 They jump over the stream. _____

6

Rewrite these sentences, adding the missing apostrophes.

> **The apostrophes are missing in contractions (when two words have been joined).**

7 Whereve they gone?

_____

8 It cant be that time already!

_____

9 We couldve gone to the cinema.

_____

10 Isnt it time we were going?

_____

11 Were going to be late.

_____

12 Well have to tell them.

_____

6

Rewrite these sentences and add the missing punctuation.

> Remember a punctuation mark (, ! or ?) needs to sit inside the speech marks.

13–15 Where is your bike asked Mrs Hill

_____

16–18 You make me laugh giggled Laura

_____

19–21 What time shall we leave asked Nazar

_____   ◯ 9

Add *did* or *done* to each sentence to make it correct.

> 'Done' usually has a helper verb nearby, for example have, has, was.

22 Sarah _____ her flute practice.

23 Olly has _____ his homework.

24 Maddie _____ a 5 km run before cycling home.

25 Some major damage has been _____ to the playground.   ◯ 4

Write whether each of these sentences is in the **past** or **present tense**.

> The form of the verb shows that something has happened (past tense) or that something is happening (present tense).

26 I am going to the shops.   _____

27 Meg listens to the music.   _____

28 I went to school.   _____

29 Tom was working at the computer.   _____

30 Jemma won the dance competition.   _____   ◯ 5

Write each of these **adverbs** in a sentence.

> An *adverb provides information on place (for example, here), time (for example, soon) or manner (for example, quickly).*

1 gently

_____

2 now

_____

3 carefully

_____

4 here

_____

5 slowly

_____

6 next

_____

6

Write a more powerful **verb** for each of these verbs.

> *A powerful verb adds more interest to your writing.*

7 ran _____

8 jump _____

9 hold _____

10 fall _____

11 give _____

12 blow _____

6

Underline the **pronouns** in the sentences.

> Pronouns take the place of a noun.

13–14 The cow chased me across the field until I escaped over a fence.

15–18 Are they sure that you put it in my bag?

19–20 He must get himself up every morning.

21–22 Watch yourselves or you will be hurt!

10

Write two examples of the following:

> Collective noun = a word referring to a group
> Verb = a doing or being word
> Connective = a word that connects two sentences or clauses
> Adjective = a word that describes a noun

23–24 a collective noun _____ _____

25–26 a verb _____ _____

27–28 a connective _____ _____

29–30 an adjective _____ _____

8

Now go to the Progress Chart to record your score! Total 30

19

Focus test 9 — Vocabulary 2

Write the **abbreviations** of these words.

> An abbreviation is a shortened form of a word or words.

1 Please turn over   _____

2 metre   _____

3 Prime Minister   _____

4 South Africa   _____

5 kilogram   _____

6 doctor   _____

6

Write the **diminutive** for the young of each of these animals.

> A diminutive is a word implying smallness.

7 duck   _____

8 goose   _____

9 owl   _____

10 pig   _____

11 bull   _____

5

Write the masculine form of these words.

> Masculine words are words that relate to males.

12 queen   _____

13 auntie   _____

14 goose   _____

15 niece   _____

16 hen   _____

17 duchess   _____

18 tigress   _____

7

Choose a word to complete each expression.

> *An expression is a way of putting an idea into words.*

music   head   leaf   rat   fence   water

19 To turn over a new _____

20 To face the _____

21 To smell a _____

22 To get into hot _____

23 To sit on the _____

24 To hang your _____

6

Write these words in alphabetical order.

> *Words arranged in the order they are found in the alphabet are in alphabetical order.*

telephone   test   taxi   target   team   terrier

25 _____

26 _____

27 _____

28 _____

29 _____

30 _____

6

Pizza ... perfect!

Pizzas smell delicious, look delicious and taste delicious.
Here is how you can make your own.

You will need: **Equipment:**
250 g self-raising flour   large oven tray
¼ teaspoon of salt   bowl
30 g butter, chopped into chunks   rolling pin
approx. 1 cup milk   kitchen brush   5
1 tbsp oil   knife
60 g tomato sauce
200 g cheddar cheese, grated
1 tomato, thinly sliced
some pineapple slices, drained and chopped into pieces   10
a slice of ham or salami, chopped

Method:
1 Turn on your oven to 210 °C or 420 °F.
2 Sift the flour and salt into the bowl. Then add the butter.
3 Using your fingertips, rub the butter and flour together. You know   15
   you are done when they look like breadcrumbs.
4 Add the milk, a little at a time. Knead and mix into a soft dough.
   More milk might be needed.
5 Roll your dough out on to the oven tray, making a large, flat circle
   of dough.   20
6 Brush the dough with the oil. Then top with the tomato sauce.
7 Now add the toppings. Arrange the cheese, tomato, pineapple and
   ham or salami on top of the pizza.
8 Bake your pizza for 25 minutes, or until cooked.

Serves 4.   25

Answer these questions.

   1 How much cheddar cheese is needed to make this pizza?

_____

2 When do you know the flour and butter have mixed together correctly?

_____

3 What do you need to do to prepare the pineapple?

_____

4–5 Why does it help to have the equipment listed? What piece of equipment is missing from the list?

_____

_____

6 Why do you think the last two ingredients don't list a specific weight?

_____

7–8 The 'You will need' list doesn't only provide a list of ingredients. List two other pieces of information it provides.

_____

_____

9 Look carefully at the listed ingredients. What do you notice about the order they are written in?

_____

10 If you were to change the topping for this pizza, which point in the method would need amending?

_____

11–13 Invent your own pizza topping, and rewrite the point or points in the method to amend the recipe.

_____

_____

_____

14–15 Look carefully at this recipe. List two ways the recipe information could be improved.

_____

_____

Add the missing *ie* or *ei* letters to complete each word correctly.

> Remember: 'i before e except after c, or when the word sound is not ee'.

1 v ____ ____ n

2 ____ ____ ght

3 pr ____ ____ st

4 th ____ ____ f

5 shr ____ ____ k

6 rec ____ ____ ve

6

Each of these words has an unstressed vowel. Write the unstressed vowel.

> An unstressed vowel is a vowel within the word that is hard to hear.

7 history   _____

8 camera   _____

9 interest   _____

10 nursery   _____

11 vegetable   _____

12 spaghetti   _____

6

Add a different **suffix** to each of these to make a new word.

> You can choose any suffix, as long as you make an actual word.

13 collect   _____

14 quick   _____

15 discuss   _____

16 short   _____

17 power   _____

18 collapse   _____

6

Answers will vary for questions that require the child to answer in their own words. Possible answers to most of these questions are given in *italics*.

Focus test 1: Spelling 1

1 second
2 tough
3 mouthful
4 giraffe
5 sandal
6 pattern
7 cow
8 church
9 box
10 horse
11 bush
12 bike
13 dishonest
14 disbelieve
15 unaware
16 discontinue
17 unimportant
18 unwell
19–24 magic, giant, storage, imagine, plunge, strange
25 childhood
26 homeless
27 entertainment
28 expensive
29 forgivable
30 loneliness

Focus test 2: Sentences 1

1 Jess loved reading the book on her shelf.
2 The window needed painting before it rained.
3 The tennis court was in use.
4 The cat played with the escaped mouse.
5 The dog was barking at the postman.
6 The sheep called to its lamb.
7–8 The sandwich had ham, cheese, pickle and tomato in it.
9–10 I must remember to take my green towel, swimming costume, clear goggles and hairbrush tonight.
11–12 Jacob loves to play football, swim, run races and sleep!

13 We are going to **S**wansea on **T**uesday.
14 **H**ave you read *The Secret Garden*?
15 **L**ook, **I** think we are flying over **M**ount **E**verest.
16 **M**iss **M**orris wants to see **F**reya and **H**arry before they go home.
17 **S**hall we go to **L**ondon to see the musical *Billy Elliot*?
18 **K**yle's birthday is in **M**arch, one month before mine.
19 The rain poured in through the open window on to the chair.
20 Tuhil forgot to write down his homework so he got into trouble.
21 The washing machine broke down, which upset my mum.
22 The dog was exhausted after his walk and slept for hours.
23 Aimee loved going to the cricket club and then walking home with her friends afterwards.
24 Simon painted the windows very carefully so paint wouldn't go on the glass.
25 ?
26 .
27 ?
28 ! (. is also correct but ! is a better answer.)
29 ! (. is also correct but ! is a better answer.)
30 .

Focus test 3: Grammar 1

1–6 Princess Caroline, Egypt, Mr Golding, January, Tooting Street, Tuesday
7 The bike skidded to a halt.
8 The blood drips from my nose.
9 I check information on the internet.
10 I lost my pencil case yesterday.
11 Tory cooks a cake every weekend.
12 The trees blew in the wind.
13 *or*
14 *and*
15 *because*
16 *as*
17 *so*
18 *until*

19–24

	Comparative adjectives	Superlative adjectives
big	bigger	biggest
small	smaller	smallest
happy	happier	happiest
sad	sadder	saddest

25 inside
26 over
27 on
28 under
29 into
30 below

Focus test 4: Vocabulary 1

1 *kind*
2 *incorrect*
3 *thin*
4 *weak*
5 *empty*
6 *boil*
7–8 *whiz, bang*
9–10 *glug, splash*
11–12 *snarl, howl*
13–18 backhand, bookmark, handshake, handmade, handbook, background
19 kitchen
20 kilometre
21 knuckles
22 kangaroo
23 kilt
24 kidney
25 France
26 Italy
27 Italy
28 France
29 USA
30 USA

Focus test 5: Comprehension 1

1 The main character of this story is a flea.
2–3 The flea considered moving to the sheep because its wool smelled nice. The flea also thought that the wool was thicker, softer and safer than the dog hair.
4 The flea wanted to avoid the dog's claws and teeth.
5–6 The flea discovered that the sheep's wool was very thick and set close together.
7 The flea needs to get to the sheep's skin to feed.
8–9 *Child's own answer describing how they think the flea might have felt. Line 19 describes the flea weeping for days, which should inform their answer.*
10–11 'Dense' means closely set together. 'Laboriously' means needing lots of effort.
12–13 *Child's own answer suggesting that the underlying message in this story is that even when things look better it doesn't necessarily mean that they are … the grass isn't always greener on the other side.*
14–15 *Child's own answer suggesting a modern-day situation, for example having one group of friends but going to play with another group because it looks more fun with them. Once with the new group, you realise that you don't like the new friends, but the old friends now don't want you with them.*

Focus test 6: Spelling 2

1 knocking
2 dragging
3 amusing
4 tricking
5 circling
6 whispering
7 weight
8 cough
9 dove
10 tongue
11 moustache
12 bruise
13 c
14 g
15 g
16 b

17 c
18 b
19 lunches
20 dishes
21 offices
22 babies
23 marbles
24 daisies
25 autograph
26 biplane
27 bicycle
28 autocue
29 autopilot
30 biannual

9 *grasp*
10 *collapse*
11 *present*
12 *gust*
13–14 The cow chased <u>me</u> across the field until <u>I</u> escaped over a fence.
15–18 Are <u>they</u> sure that <u>you</u> put <u>it</u> in <u>my</u> bag?
19–20 <u>He</u> must get <u>himself</u> up every morning.
21–22 Watch <u>yourselves</u> or <u>you</u> will be hurt!
23–24 *choir, swarm*
25–26 *hurry, eat*
27–28 *and, so*
29–30 *brown, heavy*

Focus test 7: Sentences 2

1 I enjoy reading.
2 I walk to school.
3 I eat tea at 6pm.
4 I woke up late.
5 I run fast.
6 I jump over the stream.
7 Where've they gone?
8 It can't be that time already!
9 We could've gone to the cinema.
10 Isn't it time we were going?
11 We're going to be late.
12 We'll have to tell them.
13–15 "Where is your bike**?**" asked Mrs Hill.
16–18 "You make me laugh," giggled Laura.
19–21 "What time shall we leave**?**" asked Nazar.
22 did
23 done
24 did
25 done
26 present
27 present
28 past
29 past
30 past

Focus test 8: Grammar 2

1–6 *Child's own sentences using the given adverbs correctly.*
7 *sprinted*
8 *leap*

Focus test 9: Vocabulary 2

1 PTO
2 m
3 PM
4 SA
5 kg
6 Dr
7 duckling
8 gosling
9 owlet
10 piglet
11 bullock
12 king
13 uncle
14 gander
15 nephew
16 cockerel or rooster
17 duke
18 tiger
19 leaf
20 music
21 rat
22 water
23 fence
24 head
25 target
26 taxi
27 team
28 telephone
29 terrier
30 test

Focus test 10: Comprehension 2

1. 200 g of cheddar cheese is needed to make the pizza.
2. The flour and butter have mixed together correctly when they resemble breadcrumbs.
3. The pineapple needs to be drained and chopped into pieces.
4–5. It helps to have an equipment list so you can be fully prepared. The sieve is missing from the list.
6. The last two ingredients don't list a specific weight because it isn't vital information needed to make a tasty pizza. Some cooks might like more ham and less pineapple, and so on.
7–8. The 'You will need' list also provides information on how much of the ingredient is needed and also how it needs to be prepared, for example grated, sliced.
9. The ingredients are listed in the order in which they are used during the preparation of the pizza.
10. Point 7 in the method would need amending if the topping was to change.
11–13. *Child's own invention of a pizza topping with the method written to reflect this.*
14–15. *Child's own interpretation of how the recipe information might be improved, for example pictures could be used to show the various stages and a serving suggestion could be added at the end.*

Focus test 11: Spelling 3

1. vein
2. eight
3. priest
4. thief
5. shriek
6. receive
7. o
8. e
9. e
10. e
11. e
12. a
13. *collectable*
14. *quickly*
15. *discussion*
16. *shortest*
17. *powerful*
18. *collapsible*
19–20. They're, there
21. their
22. there
23–24. There, their
25. telephone
26. circumnavigate
27. transport or teleport
28. transatlantic
29. telescope
30. television

Focus test 12: Sentences 3

1. *Mum asked where her keys were.*
2. *Dad said it is going to be hot today.*
3. *Leah asked whether you are coming to the park.*
4. *Ben wished they were going to Spain.*
5. *Mr Mead asked whether you enjoyed the lesson today.*
6. *Laith stated he was going to have an ice cream.*
7–8. The fish, which was caught in the net, struggled to escape.
9–10. Suddenly, as quick as a flash, the Olympic torch had passed the spectators before they realised it.
11. My uncle, aunt, two cousins and their dogs are coming to stay for the weekend.
12. Trees have been planted by the main road to deaden the noise, though I question what effect that will have.
13–27. "**W**hat is that noise?" asked **M**addie.
"**I**'m not sure but it is scaring me," replied **M**eena.
"**S**hall we investigate?" **M**addie suggested.

28 *There wasn't any tennis because of the weather.*

29 *They didn't sing a song to the special guest.*

30 *There weren't any rain clouds in the sky.*

Focus test 13: Grammar 3

1 abstract noun
2 proper noun
3 common noun
4 abstract noun
5 collective noun
6 proper noun
7–12 *impatiently, hurriedly, noisily, quickly, quietly, sternly*
13–14 *gleaming, white*
15–16 *broken, new*
17–18 *scruffy, muddy*
19–24 *Child's own amusing sentences, which include each of the given prepositions.*
25–30 *Three sentences, each containing two possessive pronouns.*

Focus test 14: Vocabulary 3

1 *leap*
2 *quick*
3 *polish*
4 *spongy*
5 *shift*
6 *giggle*
7 trick
8 thank
9 clean
10 thick
11 tear
12 plane
13–18 dog, grass, pillow, postage, citizen, city
19 sister
20 telephone
21 head
22 road
23 knees
24 stairs
25–30 mobile phone, jeans, brunch, astronaut, satellite, trainers

Focus test 15: Comprehension 3

1 The child was not invited to their best friend's party.

2 The best friend borrowed the child's bike without asking.

3–5 *Child's own choice of two of the listed hurtful things. Each should start with a description of why they think these are particularly hurtful.*

6–7 In the third verse, line 13 'Give you a whole packet of your favourite sweets' suggests that the best friend is beginning to try to make amends.

8 The friend accepted the best friend's apology.

9–10 *Child's response detailing how they would have reacted to the apology and why.*

11 The poem has a clear structure with repeating lines. The first line in each verse is the same or very similar each time, and each verse finishes with the words 'Mine did' until the final verse. The change at the end gives the poem a final impact.

12–13 The poet is suggesting that when someone is nasty and horrible to you, you don't need to be horrible and nasty in return.

14–15 *Child's own comment on whether they like the poem and why.*

Mixed paper 1

1 Derek Williams wrote the letter.

2 Both the school and Mr Williams' address show that they are in the same road.

3–4 The letter is complaining about the amount of litter that has been dropped and the behaviour of some of the children on their way home.

5 *Child's own opinion stating why the letter was written to the head teacher, for example because the head is in a position that could influence the children.*

6–7 It is concerning that children have been chasing the neighbour's cat as potentially the children might run out into the road and find themselves in danger and also the same might happen to the cat, as well as being a cruel thing to do.

8–9 *Child's own thoughts on why the head teacher passed the letter on to the School Council. It might have been to get ideas on how best to respond and to see the problem from the children's point of view.*

10–11 Mr Williams finds this situation concerning because it is affecting the environment in which he lives. He can see things getting worse and he has little control over what is happening.

12 'Proximity' means near to, in the same neighbourhood.

13 *Child's own response to whether a decrease in the amount of litter would mean that the other problems would be solved.*

14–15 *Child's brief description on the response they feel the head teacher should make to Mr Williams.*

16 puzzle or puddle
17 sunny
18 address
19 lesson
20 wriggle
21 lilies
22 ponies
23 countries
24 toys
25 flies
26 illegal
27 illegible
28 impossible
29 impolite
30 impatient
31 are
32 is
33 are
34–35 Is, are
36 .
37 ?

38 .
39 ! or .
40 !
41 It is time to eat tea.
42 We are going to the fair.
43 The dog needs a walk.
44 I have forgotten your birthday.
45 The lambs are resting.
46 *unattractive*
47 *arrive*
48 *dislike*
49 *forget*
50 *whisper*
51 *hairbrush*
52 *football*
53 *armchair*
54 earache
55 headband
56 lioness
57 cow
58 duck
59 sow
60 ewe
61 *eventually*
62 *grumpily*
63 *quickly*
64 *continuously*
65 *soundly*
66 *stroll*
67 *stare*
68 *strike*
69 *terrify*
70 *scribble*
71 We watched the aeroplanes <u>while</u> we were waiting for our flight.
72 The dog escaped <u>because</u> the gate had been left open.
73 The cakes still tasted lovely <u>although</u> I had dropped them on the floor.
74 It is very sunny <u>so</u> my mum always puts sun cream on my face.
75 Dan has to go to Aidan's house <u>until</u> he gets picked up.

1 The Olympics were first held in Greece.
2 The Olympics were first held in honour of the God Zeus.
3–4 *Child's own summary of the first Olympic Games including information on size, event, competitors and so on.*
5 Emperor Theodosius stopped the Olympic Games in AD 393.
6–7 This statement is false. The very first modern Olympic Games was a men-only event, but at the following Games, four years later, women were invited to take part.
8–9 *Child's answer to include the fact that the Games happen every four years in different countries but are overseen by the Olympic Committee. They cover 16 days of sporting events with as many as 205 countries taking part.*
10–11 *Child's own view on the most important value to an athlete and why that might be.*
12–13 *Child's own view on the most important value to a member of the organising committee and why that might be.*
14–15 *Child's own answer stating why the values are important and what might happen if they weren't in place, for example if equality wasn't respected some people or countries might get an advantage over others.*
16 shameful
17 carefully
18 magnetise
19 invention
20 spottiest
21 she + will
22 have + not
23 it + is
24 must + have
25 would + not
26–30 recipe, necessary, circus, prince, peace
31–34 *Two sentences, each with two commas correctly placed.*
35–37 "I love eating chocolate," said Rory.
38–40 "Are we going to get wet?" asked Naomi.
41 I went to the cinema.
42 The baby was asleep.
43 The dogs were fighting.
44 Jess loved running.
45 I stayed up late.
46 tidy
47 support
48 black
49 circle
50 legal
51 To face a difficult situation
52 To do things the wrong way around
53 To act on something at the appropriate time
54 To make something into a bigger issue than it needs to be
55 To be suspicious about something
56 *baa*
57 *cheep*
58 *grunt*
59 *miaow*
60 *cluck*
61–65 *Five prepositions, for example under, over, in, through, outside.*
66–70

Proper noun	Common noun	Collective noun	Abstract noun
Hawaii	headband	herd	hate
			happiness

71 *faster*
72 *brightest*
73 *smelliest*
74 *quicker*
75 *smarter*

1 John was walking along an old country road at night.
2 It was a very wet night, which made it hard to see any distance.
3 'the ground was sodden' means that the ground had been made very wet.

4–5 *Child's own interpretation of how John would have felt. For example: John would have felt relieved to have found shelter though scared and apprehensive as he approached.*

6 The innkeeper wasn't initially friendly though did ask him in and then catered for his needs.

7–8 John felt relieved once in the inn, 'John could have hugged him' suggests how happy John felt and then he felt comforted by how well he was looked after.

9–10 'He was tired' appears on lines 1–2, and 'his eyes dark' (line 27) and he 'fell asleep before he knew it' (line 29) suggest that John was very tired.

11–12 John could have been bewildered and confused when he woke because he had woken from a deep sleep and the room he was in was pitch black.

13 *Child's own comment on how they would have felt in the same situation John found himself.*

14–15 *Child's own suggestion on what John might have done next and why.*

16 ✓

17 x

18 x

19 x

20 ✓

21 *trough*

22 *brought*

23 *bough*

24 *dough*

25 *borough*

26 weight

27 believe

28 sleigh

29 receipt

30 chief

31 Tom's phone was lost.

32 Mimi's painting was fantastic.

33 Jake's recipe was better than expected.

34 Aimee's dog loved her.

35–45 It was a hot, **A**ugust evening. **G**ita was chatting to her friend. **"D**o you want to stay for a sleepover**?"** **G**ita asked**.**

46–47 *kind, thoughtful*

48–49 *polite, pleasant*

50–51 *remark, comment*

52 *a group of people*

53 *a living thing that has roots and grows in the earth*

54 *to sit or stand in a bent over, lazy way*

55 *having an unpleasant smell*

56 microscope

57 midnight

58 mile

59 minnow

60 mistletoe

61 his

62 scream

63 rickety

64 often

65 elastic

66 they

67 suddenly

68 steal

69–71 *Three collective nouns, for example herd, pack, choir.*

72–75 *Child's own sentence that includes a connective, an adjective, a pronoun and a preposition.*

Write 'there', 'their' or 'they're' in each gap.

> When words sound the same but are spelled differently, we call them homophones.

19–20 _____ going over _____.

21 Where are _____ coats?

22 Shall we meet them over _____?

23–24 _____ is _____ car, parked by the river.

6

Choose the correct **prefix** to complete each word.

> Remember: a prefix is a group of letters added to the beginning of the word.

tele   trans   circum

25 _____phone

26 _____navigate

27 _____port

28 _____atlantic

29 _____scope

30 _____vision

6

Write these sentences as **reported speech**.

> Reported speech is the reporting of what has been said without using the exact words or speech marks.

1   "Where are my keys?" asked Mum.

_____

2   "It is going to be hot today," said Dad.

_____

3   "Are you coming to the park?" called Leah.

_____

4   "I wish we were going to Spain," sighed Ben.

_____

5   "Did you enjoy the lesson today?" asked Mr Mead.

_____

6   "I'm going to have an ice cream," said Laith.

_____

6

Add the missing commas to these sentences.

> You need commas when there is a slight pause in the sentence or to separate items in a list.

7–8   The fish which was caught in the net struggled to escape.

9–10   Suddenly as quick as a flash the Olympic torch had passed the spectators before they realised it.

11   My uncle aunt two cousins and their dogs are coming to stay for the weekend.

12   Trees have been planted by the main road to deaden the noise though I question what effect that will have.

6

Copy the passage, adding the missing capital letters and punctuation.

Once you have copied this passage carefully, read it again to check that you haven't missed anything.

13–27 what is that noise asked maddie

i'm not sure but it is scaring me replied meena

shall we investigate maddie suggested

_____

_____

_____

_____

_____ 15

Rewrite these sentences without the double negatives.

A sentence with double negatives doesn't make sense!

28 There wasn't no tennis because of the weather.

_____

29 They didn't sing no song to the special guest.

_____

30 There weren't no rain clouds in the sky.

_____ 3

Which type of **noun** (**common**, **proper**, **abstract** or **collective**) is each of these words?

> Common noun　= a word for general people, places or things
> Proper noun　 = a word for particular people, places or things
> Abstract noun = a word referring to a concept or idea
> Collective noun = a word referring to a group

1　love 　＿＿＿＿＿＿＿＿ noun

2　Jamaica 　＿＿＿＿＿＿＿＿ noun

3　traffic light 　＿＿＿＿＿＿＿＿ noun

4　happiness 　＿＿＿＿＿＿＿＿ noun

5　flock 　＿＿＿＿＿＿＿＿ noun

6　Mrs Bradshaw 　＿＿＿＿＿＿＿＿ noun

6

Add different **adverbs** to each sentence.

> An adverb provides information on place (for example, here), time (for example, soon) or manner (for example, quickly).

7–8　The puppies waited ＿＿＿＿＿＿＿＿ as they were prepared

＿＿＿＿＿＿＿＿ for their walk.

9–10　The puppies waited ＿＿＿＿＿＿＿＿ as they were prepared

＿＿＿＿＿＿＿＿ for their walk.

11–12　The puppies waited ＿＿＿＿＿＿＿＿ as they were prepared

＿＿＿＿＿＿＿＿ for their walk.

6

Write two **adjectives** to describe each of these nouns.

> An adjective is a word that describes a noun.

13–14 lighthouse _____   _____

15–16 computer _____   _____

17–18 shoes _____   _____

6

Use each of these **prepositions** in an amusing sentence.

> A preposition can give the position of something in relation to something else.

19 under _____

20 on _____

21 inside _____

22 over _____

23 down _____

24 through _____

6

Write three sentences. Each sentence must include two possessive **pronouns**.

> A possessive pronoun is a pronoun that shows to whom something belongs, for example mine, yours.

25–26 _____

27–28 _____

29–30 _____

6

Write a **synonym** for each of these words.

> A synonym is a word with the same or similar meaning to another word.

1   jump   _____

2   fast   _____

3   clean   _____

4   soft   _____

5   move   _____

6   laugh   _____

6

Underline the **root word** for each of these words.

> A root word is the word to which prefixes and suffixes are added to make another word.

7   tricked

8   thankful

9   unclean

10   thicken

11   tearfully

12   biplane

6

Circle the words that are not **homophones**.

> Homophones are words that have the same sound as another word but a different meaning or spelling.

13–18	break	four	bear	dog
	key	dye	grass	pillow
	postage	citizen	frieze	buy
	city	new	there	course

6

With a line, match the cockney rhyming slang dialect words with their meaning.

> A dialect word is a word that is particular to a specific region of the country.

19	skin and blister	head
20	dog and bone	sister
21	lump of lead	stairs
22	frog and toad	knees
23	bread and cheese	telephone
24	apples and pears	road

6

Circle six words that have entered our language in the last 150 years.

> New words are constantly being added to our language to describe new things and ideas as they are created.

25–30	mobile phone	horse	jeans	brunch
	dinner	astronaut	year	milk
	satellite	coat	trainers	ball

6

Best Friends

Would a best friend
Eat your last sweet
Talk about you behind your back
Have a party and not ask you?
Mine did.   5

Would a best friend
Borrow your bike without telling you
Deliberately forget your birthday
Avoid you whenever possible?
Mine did.   10

Would a best friend
Turn up on your bike
Give you a whole packet of your favourite sweets
Look you in the eye?
Mine did.   15

Would a best friend say
Sorry I talked about you behind your back
Sorry I had a party and didn't invite you
Sorry I deliberately forgot your birthday
– I thought you'd fallen out with me?   20
Mine did.

And would a best friend say, simply,
Never mind
That's OK?
I did.   25

Bernard Young

Answer these questions.

1   The best friend had a party. Why was this a problem?

   _____

2   What did the best friend borrow without permission?

   _____

3–5 The best friend does a number of hurtful things. Choose the two you would find most hurtful and explain why.

_____

_____

_____

6–7 In which verse does the best friend begin to try to make amends? Copy the line from the poem.

_____

_____

8 The best friend apologised. How did the friend react to this apology?

_____

9–10 Would you have reacted to the apology in the same way? Why?

_____

_____

_____

11 What do you notice about how this poem is written? What lines are repeated?

_____

12–13 What message do you think the poet is writing through this poem?

_____

_____

_____

14–15 Do you like this poem? Why?

_____

_____

_____

This letter arrived first thing on Wednesday morning.

Mr Farrow passed it on to the School Council, asking the members what they thought he should do.

Knightley Close
Toddingworth
Kent
BR14 9HB

Mr Farrow   5
Head teacher of Headley Primary School
Knightley Close
Toddingworth
Kent
BR14 9HB   Tuesday 18 May   10

Dear Mr Farrow,

I hope you don't mind me writing but I now feel that I have no option.
    We live in close proximity to your school and have enjoyed seeing
the children come and go over many years.
    Unfortunately, recently, we have noticed an increasing amount of   15
litter being left after the children have made their way home. We feel
this is now having an adverse effect on the look of the area.
    Also, the more litter that is dropped the less care the children
seem to be taking over other things. We often have to ask children
to stop climbing on our small wall at the front of the house and we   20
have even seen children chasing our neighbour's cat into the road.
Obviously all of this is very concerning.
    While I realise the children aren't at school while causing these
problems, I feel it appropriate to write to you with our concerns.

Yours sincerely,   25

Derek Williams
Mr D Williams

Answer these questions.

1 Who wrote this letter?

_____

2 What information do the two addresses provide us with?

_____

3–4 What is the letter complaining about?

_____

_____

5 Why do you think the letter was written to the head teacher, even though the problem wasn't happening during the school day?

_____

6–7 Give two reasons why it is concerning that some children have been seen chasing a neighbour's cat.

_____

_____

8–9 Why do you think the head teacher passed the letter on to the School Council to think about?

_____

_____

10–11 Why does Mr Williams write, 'Obviously all of this is very concerning.' (line 21)?

_____

_____

12 In the context of the letter, what does 'proximity' (line 13) mean?

_____

13 Do you think that if there was less litter the other problems would be solved?

_____

14–15 How would you respond to the letter if you were the head teacher?

_____

_____

_____

15

Add the missing double letters to each of these words.

16 pu _____ _____ le   **17** su _____ _____ y

18 a _____ _____ ress   **19** le _____ _____ on

20 wri _____ _____ le

5

Write the **plural** form of each of these **nouns**.

21 lily   _____

22 pony   _____

23 country   _____

24 toy   _____

25 fly   _____

5

Add the **prefix** *im* or *il* to each of these words.

26 _____legal

27 _____legible

28 _____possible

29 _____polite

30 _____patient

5

Add *is* or *are* to each sentence to make it correct.

31 When _____ we going to the football?

32 What _____ the time?

33 We usually _____ the loudest supporters.

34–35 _____ it likely we _____ going to win?

5

Add the missing punctuation marks.

36 You are coming to my house for tea_____

37 Can I play in goal_____

38 The bird sat quietly on its nest_____

39 Here I come_____

40 Quick, I'm going to drop it_____

5

Write these questions as statements.

41 Is it time to eat tea?

_____

42 Are we going to the fair?

_____

43 Does the dog need a walk?

_____

44 Have I forgotten your birthday?

_____

45 Are the lambs resting?

_____ **5**

Write an **antonym** for each of these words.

46 attractive _____

47 leave _____

48 like _____

49 remember _____

50 shout _____ **5**

Extend each of these words into a **compound word**.

51 hair_____

52 foot_____

53 arm_____

54 ear_____

55 head_____ **5**

Write the female equivalent of each of these creatures.

56 lion _____

57 bull _____

58 drake _____

59 boar _____

60 ram _____

Complete each sentence using a different **adverb**.

61 Zoe _____ finished her story.

62 The farmer _____ chased the bull out the yard.

63 The teacher told the children to move _____.

64 The swimmer worked _____ on improving her stroke.

65 The child slept _____ in her bed.

Write a more powerful **verb** for each of these verbs.

66 walk _____

67 look _____

68 touch _____

69 scare _____

70 write _____

Underline the **connectives** in each sentence.

71 We watched the aeroplanes while we were waiting for our flight.

72 The dog escaped because the gate had been left open.

73 The cakes still tasted lovely although I had dropped them on the floor.

74 It is very sunny so my mum always puts sun cream on my face.

75 Dan has to go to Aidan's house until he gets picked up.

The Olympic Games, an interview

When did the Olympic Games first start?
The Olympics were first held in Olympia, Greece thousands of years ago.
They were founded in honour of the God Zeus and were used to build
good relationships between cities in Greece. The only event was held on
one day, which was a men's running race. Women were allowed to   5
watch but only if they were unmarried. As time went on, more events
were included and the Games lasted for more than one day.

Have the Olympic Games been running since then?
No, it is believed the Olympic Games were stopped by Emperor Theodosius
in AD 393.   10

Who restarted the Olympic Games?
A Frenchman, Baron Pierre do Coubertin, restarted the Olympic Games in
1896. It took him two years, after putting together an Olympic Committee, to
plan and organise the event.

Were the Olympic Games in 1896 the same as they are today?   15
The first 'new' Olympic Games were held in Athens, Greece. A total of
241 athletes took part from 14 countries. All of the competitors were men.

When did women first compete in the Olympic Games?
Women competed for the first time in the 1900 Olympic Games held in Paris.

How often are the Olympic Games held?   20
The Olympic Games are held every four years. They move from country
to country but are overseen by an Olympic Committee. The Olympic Games
now last for 16 days and many, many competitors compete in approximately
26 Olympic sports from 205 different countries.

Why are the Olympic Games so important?   25
The Olympic Games are the biggest world event held. The following
values are behind everything the Olympic Games and the athletes taking
part strive for:
  • friendship
  • courage
  • determination   30
  • excellence
  • equality
  • respect
  • inspiration.   35

Answer these questions.

1 In which country were the Olympics first held?

_____

2 Why were the Olympics first created?

_____

3-4 In your own words, describe the first Olympic Games.

_____

_____

5 Who stopped the Olympic Games?

_____

6-7 'The modern Olympic Games has always included women.' Is this statement true or false? Explain your answer.

_____

_____

8-9 How are the modern Olympic Games now organised?

_____

_____

10-11 As an athlete, which of the values listed do you think is the most important and why?

_____

_____

12-13 As a member of the organising committee, which of the values listed do you think is the most important and why?

_____

_____

14-15 Why is it so important that the Olympics have the values listed in place? What might happen if they weren't thought to be important?

_____

_____

_____

15

Complete the word sums. Watch out for the spelling changes!

16 shame + ful = _____

17 careful + ly = _____

18 magnet + ise = _____

19 invent + ion = _____

20 spotty + est = _____

5

Write the words each of these **contractions** is made with.

21 she'll   = _____ + _____

22 haven't = _____ + _____

23 it's   = _____ + _____

24 must've = _____ + _____

25 wouldn't = _____ + _____

5

Circle the words that have a soft *c*.

26–30 recipe   cotton   necessary   crumb

　　　　circus   prince   collage   peace

5

Write two sentences. Each sentence needs to have two commas.

31–32 _____

33–34 _____

4

Rewrite these sentences, adding the missing punctuation.

35–37 I love eating chocolate said Rory

_____

38–40 Are we going to get wet asked Naomi

_____

6

Rewrite these sentences in the **past tense**.

41 I am going to the cinema.

_____

42 The baby is asleep.

_____

43 The dogs are fighting.

_____

44 Jess loves running.

_____

45 I am staying up late.

_____ ◯ 5

Underline the **root word** for each of these words.

46 untidy

47 supportive

48 blacken

49 semicircle

50 illegal ◯ 5

Using a line, match each expression with its meaning.

51 To face the music   To be suspicious about something

52 To put the cart before the   To act on something at the
    horse   appropriate time

53 To strike while the iron is hot   To face a difficult situation

54 To make a mountain out of   To make something into a bigger
    a molehill   issue than it needs to be

55 To smell a rat   To do things the wrong way around ◯ 5

Write an **onomatopoeic** word for the sound that each of these animals makes.

56 sheep   _____

57 bird   _____

58 pig   _____

59 cat   _____

60 hen   _____   ⬤ 5

List five **prepositions**.

61–65 _____   _____   _____

_____   _____   ⬤ 5

Complete the table with the **nouns**.

Hawaii   hate   herd

headband   happiness

66–70

Proper noun	Common noun	Collective noun	Abstract noun

⬤ 5

Add a different **adjective** of comparison to each sentence.

71 Hannah was _____ than Heath.

72 Jake is the _____ in the group.

73 This cheese was the _____ in the shop.

74 The cat was _____ than the mouse.

75 Callie was always _____ than her sister.   ⬤ 5

It was a dark night and John was walking along an old country road. He was tired and the rain was beating down on his face. Where would he spend the night? He couldn't sleep out here in the rain, and the ground was sodden. On he walked. Again and again, he lifted his head into the rain and tried to make out the shape of a hut or a house. Nothing. But then, after what 5 seemed hours, he noticed a dark hump by the side of the road that could be a house. And, indeed, the closer he walked, the more it took on the shape of the house. But at the same time, the nearer he stepped, the more strange and forbidding it seemed. High, dark, no lights.

He heard his feet on the stone path and after a moment's pause he 10 pounded on the door with his hand. A light came on in the window above and then followed the sound of feet on the stairs. The bolts banged back, one at the top, one at the bottom, and the key turned in the lock. When the door opened, John could make out a great slab of a man.

"What do you want?" he said. 15

"I seem to have lost my way," said John, "and I would be most obliged if you'd let me have a place to lie down for the night."

"Well, you've found the right place here," said the man. "This is an inn."

John felt a warm wave travel down his back and he saw himself passing through the luxuries of a hot bath, soft towels, hot soup, a roaring fire, a 20 soft bed.

"Step right in," said the man.

John could have hugged him.

And indeed, it was just as he had imagined: the bath, the towels, the soup, the fire and the bed. 25

Just before he settled down for the night, John looked around the room. He caught sight of himself in the mirror, his eyes dark and tired. He draped his clothes over a chair and hung his old rucksack on a hook on the wall and fell asleep before he knew it.

A couple of hours later he woke up. The room was pitch black. He 30 scarcely knew he had opened his eyes. He lay there for a moment wondering why he had woken up – then slowly he realized he could smell smoke. He sniffed the cold air. That was most definitely smoke. John lay in his bed staring into the blackness. Smoke … smoke … he said the word over in his mind not thinking what it really meant until quite suddenly it 35 joined another word – fire? He felt gripped with terror.

From *The Hook* by Michael Rosen

Answer these questions.

1 Where was John at the beginning of this passage?

_____

2 Describe the weather.

_____

3 What is meant by 'the ground was sodden' (line 3)?

_____

4–5 Describe how you think John felt when he found the house.

_____

_____

6 Was the innkeeper welcoming?

_____

7–8 How did John feel once in the inn? Use evidence to support your answer.

_____

_____

9–10 Write two pieces of evidence from the passage that illustrate that John was very tired.

_____

_____

11–12 Give two reasons why you think John felt so bewildered and confused when he woke up.

_____

_____

13 How would you feel if you were John and found yourself in the same situation in the middle of the night?

_____

_____

14–15 What do you think John will do next? Why?

_____

_____

_____

15

Put a tick next to the words spelled correctly and a cross next to those spelled incorrectly.

16 exercise ☐

17 experiance ☐

18 secretry ☐

19 possesion ☐

20 permanent ☐

5

Next to each word, write another word with the same letter string making the same sound.

21 cough _____

22 thought _____

23 plough _____

24 though _____

25 thorough _____

5

Add the missing _ie_ or _ei_ letters to complete each word correctly.

26 w ____ ____ ght   **27** bel ____ ____ ve

28 sl ____ ____ gh   **29** rec ____ ____ pt

30 ch ____ ____ f

5

Rewrite these sentences, adding the missing apostrophes showing possession.

31 Toms phone was lost.

_____

32 Mimis painting was fantastic.

_____

33 Jakes recipe was better than expected.

_____

34 Aimees dog loved her.

_____ ⭘ 4

Rewrite the following correctly.

35–45 it was a hot august evening gita was chatting to her friend
do you want to stay for a sleepover gita asked

_____

_____

_____

_____ ⭘ 11

Write two **synonyms** for each word.

46–47 nice   _____   _____

48–49 good   _____   _____

50–51 say   _____   _____ ⭘ 6

Write a definition for each of these words.

52 crowd   _____

53 plant   _____

54 slouch   _____

55 pungent _____ ⭘ 4

Write these words in **alphabetical order**.

minnow   mile   microscope   mistletoe   midnight

56 _____   **57** _____

58 _____   **59** _____

60 _____ ⭘ 5

Circle the word that is:

61	a pronoun	until	over	his	although
62	a verb	slowly	under	they	scream
63	an adjective	rickety	jump	hate	through
64	an adverb	itself	often	fierce	crawl
65	an adjective	dinosaur	under	elastic	them
66	a pronoun	slimy	man	yesterday	they
67	an adverb	he	knee	suddenly	attack
68	a verb	giraffe	steal	upwards	around

○ 8

Write three **collective nouns**.

69–71 _____ _____ _____

○ 3

Write a sentence that includes a **connective**, an **adjective**, a **pronoun** and a **preposition**.

72–75 _____

_____

○ 4